Guttural

Pyretta Kaiser

Presentation by *BookLeaf Publishing*

Web: www.bookleafpub.com

E-mail: info@bookleafpub.com

ISBN: 9789357443142

First edition 2023

*To Grey. I shared my breath, I shared my blood,
but I could not share my strength.*

ACKNOWLEDGEMENT

Thank you to my loved ones for their advice, support, and love.
A special thank you to Victoria and Elysia.

PREFACE

I wrote these poems to bring to life the things I can't say out loud. These poems are very important to me, and I hope some of them might become important to you too, in whatever way you might need.

Stagnant

With enough time all will be new
The outside world will move on quickly and
without remorse
And we will remain encapsulated within this
ageless chamber
Plastic, ever breathing against the stillness
You exist tenderly in the hollow of my throat
Time could never dream of stealing you away
from me
I will forever keep you between myself and the
earth
My precious gem, my agony

Blind

During times like these you don't seem real
With my face pressed so firmly to the glass my
conjunctiva fogs my view
I can barely make out your image
As if the gods have boxed my ears and blinded
me
I sit warmly numb beside your outline
Shimmering apparition, darling one
The knife forever pressed against my throat feels
instead as if it will phase through me
I long hopelessly for its bite
For the bite is much preferable to the haze laid
heavily upon my eyes

Covet

I want to tear his heart from his chest and wear it
around my neck
To feel his affections spill down the front of me
Running down my abdomen and thighs and
pooling at my feet
To relish in the warmth of him
The bitter, metallic taste of him clinging to the
back of my nose and throat
I would cherish my stained fingers and palms
Divinity in essence
Pure expression of my devotion
Through my claws he will feel my love

Beguiled

So sweet the love dripping from my lashes
Your plum stained lips sit open waiting for me
Sit back and hold my breath against you as your
cherry knife glides through me with all the
confidence of someone who's done this before
I bare my teeth against your skin in ever present
threat and adoration
You coo gently into the clouds above me
The words so heavily pregnant with artificial
tenderness they drop fat onto my eyes

Enraptured

The flowers from your eyes have planted seeds
in mine, roots creeping and curling into me and
making their home among the wreckage
Soon my faults and weaknesses will reveal
themselves to both of us, clinging to us like a
throbbing cancer intent on destruction
You glow subdued and soft beneath my serrated
claws, your decorated hands slowly unlacing and
loosening my skin like the leather of your old
boots
My bones fall slack against you with such
sickening sweetness I fear my veins may peel
themselves from my body
You breathe acid fondness into me
I dissolve beneath your starving touch

Burnt Sugar

You disgust me
Revolting
I recoil at your presence
Your aroma wafts like roses blistered in the sun,
burnt sugar and wet dirt
You're caught in my throat and I do my best to
claw you out, soil caked beneath my nails and
cracking callus
Your voice splits my skull in two with vicious
precision, digging talons into grey matter
Your name sits like razor blades against my
tongue
I can only speak sweetly

Infection

The taste of your name still stains my every
exhale
Billowing up from the bubbling pit of my
insides like fungal spores
It infects my every crevice
Invading the book lungs of my arachnid body
with merciless brutality

Burn

I wish I could tattoo the image of you to my
dreams, to stitch you to the flesh of my
unconscious mind
I feel you drifting ever further, it's almost been a
year
I fear one day I'll truly be without you, that the
gods won't allow me even sparkling
hallucination
I fear a phantom will come once more to remove
you from my exhausted arms, muscles strained
against the weight of memory
One day surely I'll burn straight through this
bed, through the sheets and mattress directly into
the earth below
This weight in my chest grows heavier each time
you brush past the back of my mind
I'm sure one day it will drown me

Invidious

With ease you pass into the heavens
Softly your breath rattles through your physical
form upon your graceful exit
So sweet, the kiss of death
Laid gently upon your temple
Upon your eyes and palms
With grief and writhing misery the rest will
follow
I envy you
For such long life comes not without
consequence
Without curse and lurking misery
The gods have long since abandoned us
Forced forever to wander the waking world
A corpse among the living
Ever dreaming of that final step from shadow
into white hot, burning ecstasy
But there is no heaven above me
No great master to return to
I am damned to this purgatory
Forever feeding upon the greedy lips of the
living
How I wish I could be greedy
How I wish I could kiss death

Splinters

You break my heart into a million
Tiny
Little pieces
They form ulcers down my throat and into my
stomach
That bleed only for you
The sharpest pieces stick fast beneath my tongue
And hold my whispers hostage
Sick with desire
I ache for you sharply between my joints
Long for you between every layer of my skin
Your idealized form rests heavy around the
curves of my body
I hold your words within the cracks of my palm
and watch as they drop and fall to the ground
Is this exactly what I wanted?
Maybe I'm just taking what I can get

Between my lungs

Such cruelty it is to exist in this way
To ache and groan with empty bones and center
To long for a part of me since destroyed and torn
away
How I wish I could return to my prior state
But I soon would regret it
For then I would truly be without you
Your cells would no longer flow through my
cold blood
Through my heart and between my lungs
You would cease to exist entirely
But I'm not sure which is worse

Rat

You exist forever in my periphery
With hushed voice you still call out to me
Vivid and out of reach
You take from me what I took from you
Am I still demanding space within your skull?
Do I still press my palms to the inner lining of
your brain with as much vigor and aggression as
you do mine?
I can only hope
I hope we still exist intertwined within the space
between us
Sometimes I feel as if I could almost reach out
and feel your gentle palm against the tips of my
fingers and taste the scent of your distress within
the walls of my throat

Fawn

I wish to envelope myself within him
To take up residence in the tender lining of his
consciousness
The warmth and tightness of his skin becoming
more familiar than my own
I wish I could hide inside of his body
For him to become my hermit crab shell
I want nothing more
For inside the hollow of another is the only place
I find reprieve
To live my life a parasite
Feeding upon his affections
I wish I could eat him alive

Specimen

Your gaze traps me, frozen in time I am a
delicate specimen under your glass
You slide your paper underneath me yet refuse
to set me free
You pull and pin my desiccated body, contorting
me to your delight
You've removed my insides
Replacing them with paper kisses and cotton
whispers
Lovingly you enclose me in your frame

Creatures

Lay with me in the night, existing only beneath
the dimmed stars and moon
Sit here in the dark with me among my
creatures, listen to the chattering of mandibles
on decaying vegetation and prey
Let your skin crawl with delight as they make
their nightly rounds, gathering all you thought
you'd left behind
Among them I find my peace, within their soil I
make my home among the springtails
With me, my wet earth and complex burrows
You could stay
Don't mind the spiders, for their touch is tender
and their paws are gentle
Let their webs keep us connected
Fear not the mantis, she surely will pay you no
mind
Gaze upon her praying arms in awe and envy
Exist within my world for just a bit longer
Turn towards all you thought you'd abhor, for we
only have our love to give
Rot with me, my darling, let our remains not go
to waste

Moth

You rip my chest open just to take a peek
Ribs snapping between your fingers like the
pencils I used to write your name on the roof of
my mouth
You drop your sugar water into me through
chewed lips
It fills me to the top of my throat
I wish you could crawl inside me or I could
crawl out
It is within you I find the warmth my hands have
been searching for
Out of reach and burning, it scorches the tips of
my fingers
I know if I get too close you'll set me ablaze
Yet I continue like a moth to flame
Soon you'll burn my dusted wings to nothing
and I will accept my fate
Wounded and listless in the palms of your hands

Teeth

You taught me to keep my complaints inside
Tucked into the spaces between my gums and
teeth like strands of meat
I can feel them as they sit and rot, forming
cavities in the creases of my mind
You push and pull me as if I were a loose molar
you couldn't wait to knock from your skull
Each time you nudged and stabbed the aching
gingiva, I found that less and less of me
remained within my borrowed body

Garnet

My body aches for the warmth it once held
All the hope and sin mustered into a clump of
cells
The misgivings scraped from the walls of my
consciousness and hastily thrown into a pit of
blood and forgiveness
I am not what I once was
The entrails exposed and slithering as I claw
myself open
Nails split and bleeding
The anniversary is approaching
You should've been here
Left to rot and wither, I clutch my pulsing
viscera

Primal

Complex spaces left unprotected
Ripped to pieces with selfish carelessness
Invaded poked and prodded
Never the same
I never got to see you
Did I?
You haunt me
I am disgusted
The primal ache and yearning
Never buried
Forever mourning
I wish I could have touched you

Molder

It tore the heart from my body
The wound radiates vibrant longing
It burns the backs of our eyes
The liquid warmth flows from the tips of my
fingers into the pits below
The drip drip dripping sound of heartache
reverberates through your avian bones
We step back and sit just beneath the heavens
Too far to reach but close enough to imagine
This is no place for us
The match struck against your spine burns so
brightly we can't help but whimper in awe
The fumes will soon overtake us
We melt against each other, salted fat and sugar

A moment

It takes everything in me not to tear down these
walls
To rip the wiring from the insides and tear the
floors apart
I sit in exhaustion and quiet panic
I take my breath at every chance and bottle it
Save it for later
For emergencies only
Yes I am not allowed to breathe
Not now
Not until I truly need it
In this way I've kept us safe
Kept my head above the raging and roaring
waters
Kept you pressed tightly against my sternum
beneath paper skin
It takes everything in me
I'm tired of waiting
Tired of longing and regret
It would only take a moment
Just a second
A few minutes perhaps
It would all be over
And I would be free
It would only take a second

9 789357 443142